ACK

This book is dedicated to all
from the author's research.
over what to include in this
provided by Messrs Docherty and Roberts.

Thanks to the following:

Ken, Tony, Bill and Bob, the printers who took on this mammoth task and succeeded and through doing so have now placed an order for a new John Bull outfit.

To Paul Nicholson, for the cover background, despite being given the wrong dimensions.

To The Daily Mirror for photographs (it's obvious they haven't missed them yet!)

To all the famous people who have contributed to this book, especially Derek Dougan for his sense of humour.

CONTENTS

FOREWORD BY IAN ST JOHN

When I heard that Tommy Docherty was writing a book, my first thought was, 'How does he find the time?', because he's never been content sitting on the sideline. His involvement in football was one of the busiest I've ever known, only surpassed by his after dinner career. The Doc will undoubtedly go down in sporting history as one of the game's most colourful characters. People either love him or hate him, the latter being definitely in the minority.

He's always been his own man, as many a football chairman will testify. His retirement from football marks the end of an era, although I'm sure his presence on football panels will ensure that the 'Docherty comment' will continue for many years. And now for my personal view of the man.

I've known Tommy for more years than I care to remember. In fact, our careers did overlap when I was selected for young Scotland and the Doc was nearing the end of his international career. Funny thing is, he now claims to be younger than me! In all that time I've never known him to be stuck for a word. Or, for that matter, a practical joke!

Early on in my career I had the dubious honour of sharing a taxi with the Doc. Or I should say, almost. We were supposed to join the other players and being young and relatively inexperienced I chose to follow instead of ask. Tommy hailed a passing taxi and jumped in. I followed. He then made a quick exit from the opposite door and climbed into a taxi behind, leaving me alone. As Tommy roared off my driver looked at me and asked, 'Where to?' I hadn't the faintest idea. All I could do was to mutter the immortal phrase, 'Follow that cab!'

If you sat down and found the absence of a chair, one thing was certain. The Doc was behind it.

Something I've always admired about him is his great determination. I remember a game we played against Northern Ireland when they fielded a tough player called Wilbur Cush. We had the equally hard Tommy Docherty. Throughout the ninety minutes neither would give an inch. They both left the field looking like they'd just gone ten rounds with Mike Tyson.

One incident highlights his sense of humour. It was a televised game at Wolves where Tommy took the unprecendented step of allowing a mobile camera in the dressing room. It was a courageous thing to do but he was always a media man, always willing to help the press and TV people. He was filmed before the game chatting to each player in turn. He came to the goalkeeper and asked how he felt. The goalie replied, 'A bit nervous, Boss.' To which the Doc turned to the camera, shrugged and said, 'That's all I need. A nervous goalkeeper!'

That's what we've come to expect from Tommy Docherty. A quick answer or flippant remark. Long may he continue to give them on the after dinner circuit.

PROLOGUE

To the young players of today I'm regarded as an ex-football manager who gives after dinner speeches. Some older members of the audience might even remember me as a player, if any are still alive that is. I once said: 'I've had more clubs than Jack Nicklaus ', which happens to be true.

This book isn't about my career in football, but about the profession that many ex-sportsmen choose to follow, that of after dinner speaker. But in case some of you have spent the last twenty years on a desert island with a Jap sniper for company, I'll start with a brief outline of my life in football.

MY CAREER
(Or how to insult a Football Chairman without really trying)

Life hasn't always been easy. I started out as a kid in Glasgow playing for two local teams, St Paul's Boy's Guild and St Mark's School. Like most kids in Glasgow at that time, we kicked anything that moved, including each other.

We used to play two matches every Saturday. St Mark's in the morning and the Boy's Guild in the afternoon, the latter being a Catholic team run by the Church. Someone asked me recently if I'd always been a Catholic. I said, "Yes, until I saw the 'Thorn Birds' a few years ago."

Now I've a reputation for not always seeing eye to eye with football chairmen. But the Boy's Guild was different. It was run by Father Joseph Connolly, our local priest, and a man who'd make Chelsea's Ken Bates look like Mother Theresa. This is where I first gained experience in leadership. As Captain, knocking up the team for early morning mass on Sunday. For if you missed that you didn't play.

Being a Catholic my greatest ambition was to play for Celtic. In those days Celtic would open up the gates about 20 minutes from the end and this enabled us to nip in to watch a game for nothing.

FATHER JOSEPH CONNELLY

A few years later I was rescued by the Army for National Service. I was in the H.L.I. ' Hitlers last issue ', or as it was officially known, the Highland Light Infantry. I was still playing football during my service and began to attract attention. When I eventually left I had the choice of signing for Newcastle or Burnley but then realised my ambition when I signed for Celtic. Unfortunately for me, a great player called Bobby Evans occupied the same position. This meant I couldn't get into the team.

About a year later the Chairman, Mr Bob Kelly, sent for me and told me I was being transferred to Preston North End for £3,000 because he felt I wouldn't make the grade at Celtic. This proved to be my first disagreement with a Chairman. Did he not think me good enough? He replied: 'No, you're not big enough!' I left that week. The following week they signed Bobby Collins, who incidentally, was about ten inches shorter than me!

So I found myself at Preston North End alongside the great Tom Finney, who I still consider to be the greatest player of all time. We were christened ' The plumber and the ten leaks ' because Tom was a plumber by trade. In fact, all the players in those days had a full time job. Not on TV panels like we see today, but proper jobs. Coal miners, tradesmen, lorry drivers, you name it and they did it.

This brought about my second disagreement with a Chairman. There was a maximum wage of fourteen pounds a week. Fourteen pounds! I've paid more than that to get my car cleaned! Tom Finney was on the maximum all year round. I was on fourteen pounds in the winter but dropped to eight pounds in the summer.

The following year I got my tenth cap for Scotland so I went to see the manager. I asked him for the same deal of fourteen pounds throughout the year. He said: 'But you're not as good a player as Finney.' I replied: 'I am in the summer.'

I was soon to realise my playing career would not end at Preston when I was transferred to Arsenal for £30,000 on August 14th, 1958. I spent three happy years at Highbury despite their strict regime. They made the Royal Marines look like a hippy outing to Stonehenge.

The end came at the age of thirty-two. I had always intended retiring at the top so I applied for a coaching job at Chelsea. The Chairman, Joe Meers, said to me: ' Tom, you're no doubt aware that we're looking for a coach. '

I replied: 'I saw you last Saturday Mr Chairman, and believe me, it isn't a coach you need, it's a hearse!'

Then he said a strange thing for a Chairman. He said: ' Tom, as Chairman of the club I know nothing about football. And the other five here know a damn sight less. ' Now this must be unique. A Chairman admitting he knows nothing about football!

The manager was Ted Drake. On our very first meeting Ted said to me: ' Tom, I just want you to know that you weren't my choice. ' Which wasn't very encouraging.

The following month of January saw me appointed as team manager. But in Joe Meers, we had a marvellous man. Unfortunately for me, and football in general, Mr Meers died and was succeeded by a man named Pratt who'd been a Chairman for twenty five years and still knew nothing. At our first board meeting I said to him, 'Mr Chairman, when I want your advice I'll give it to you.'

A week later I was on my way out of Chelsea.

During my time at Stamford Bridge, we won the League Cup, now the Littlewoods Cup and promotion back to the first division in our first season. We were never out of the top three in the first division all the time I was there and lost in the Cup Final of 1967 to Tottenham 3-1.

A TYPICAL VOTE OF CONFIDENCE FROM A FOOTBALL CHAIRMAN

'Don't worry about the result. The board is right behind you.'

I also joined Rotherham in 1967, a wonderful little club. Mainly because they only had three directors.

I made a promise I'd take them out of the second division, and I did. I took them into the third. But we did make it to the fifth round of the FA Cup. The Sunday before the match I had the players lined up on the pitch and began introducing them to an old chap wearing a bowler hat. The Chairman came down and asked what I was doing. I said, 'I'm getting the lads used to Wembley so that when they meet the King they won't be nervous.' He said, 'But it's the Queen at Wembley,' I said, 'I know, but by the time we get there it'll be the King again!'

The Chairman had the bright idea of putting the players on a bonus system of twenty five pounds a win! He lost so much money that whenever our lads pushed up past the half way line he'd stand up and shout, 'Offside!!'

Then I got my famous hat-trick at Queens Park Rangers. I was appointed manager three times! Somebody asked me if I'd ever won the 'Manager of the Month' at QPR. How could I? I wasn't there a month! Mind you, in 1968 I lasted twenty eight days, and won a miniature bottle for 'Bells Manager of the Week'.

'We got the idea for revolving doors after Tommy Docherty came back for the third time'.

My next move was to Aston Villa on the invitation of Chairman Doug Ellis. Doug told me not to worry, he was right behind me. I replied, 'I don't want you behind me. I want you in front where I can see you!' But I've got to say in his defence, Doug Ellis was the most consistent man I've ever met. He caused trouble *wherever* he went.

After my exit from Villa in 1969 I flew off to Portugal and a contract with Oporto. I offered to do my best for the club and also to adapt to local life. The Portugese newspapers acclaimed my arrival with headlines reading, 'Mr Docherty to learn Portugese by next year'. I thought to myself, that's providing I can learn English before the end of this one.'

Portugal was a wonderful place. Sunshine, miles of sandy beaches, excellent sea food. Makes you wonder why I left to go to Hull.

The reason was simple, Terry Neil was player manager and I was asked to be his coach. In fact, during one game against a Japanese eleven I actually substituted Terry because he wasn't playing well. Needless to say we could smile about it afterwards. I wasn't to spend much longer at the club but it could have been even less after my ill timed substitution.

I then received one of the games highest accolades, when in 1970 I was apponted Manager of Scotland. I had the great honour of playing for, captaining and managing my country. I had players like Denis Law who was coming to the end of his career. I also gave a first cap to an up and coming young lad. His name was Kenny Daglish.

In 1972 I was offered the job I always felt I'd been destined for, manager of Manchester United. I knew I'd been chosen for the job at Old Trafford when I saw the white smoke coming out of the boardroom window.

I remember signing a big lad called Jim Holton for £80,000 Harry Gregg, who sold Jim to us said, 'Tom, this lad doesn't know the meaning of the word defeat!' I phoned Harry back next week and said, 'Harry. It's not the only word he doesn't know the meaning of!'

With Manchester United I lost the FA Cup to Southampton in 1976 and won it against Liverpool the following year. The Liverpool match was refereed by Clive Thomas, who'd had more bookings that year than 'Thomas Cook'.

During my time at Old Trafford I had a player called George Best. People often ask if I had any trouble handling George, but I can honestly say I didn't. Mainly because he was never there!

Regardless of Liverpool's achievements I still consider Manchester United to be the biggest club in the country and the most desirable to manage.

In 1977, after five years as manager, off I set for Derby County. Derby was a steady period in my life. We never won anything but weren't relegated.

Then it was back to Queens Park Rangers for the second time. In fact, we were doing well. We'd just beaten Burnley 7-0 and were top of the second division. My contract had expired which is most unusual for me, when the chairman, Jim Gregory, sent for me. I thought to myself, successful club, new contract, must be a raise in salary. So I entered Jim's office to find the champagne flowing Jim went out for ten minutes so I helped myself to a glass of bubbly. When he returned he toasted me and said, 'Well Tom, I think it's the parting of the ways,' I said, 'Don't go Mr Chairman, I think you're doing a grand job.' He replied, 'I'm not going, Tom. You are. You're sacked.'

Later that week, Jim said there'd been a mistake and I was re-engaged. But it didn't last long. A couple of months later Jim Gregory saved face and sacked me again! During this time I'd bought a caravan which was handy for moving the family from job to job. In fact we had two jobs and a fortnights holiday in the one month!

In 1981 I tried something completely different when I flew out to Australia, taking over Sydney Olympic football club on a part time basis. There's only one trouble with Aussie grounds, you've got to move the sheep off the pitch before the match can start. I think we'd have won more games if we'd left them on!

I've never understood why Ron Atkinson never tried it out there. He could have watched the game and got a suntan at the same time.

RON ATKINSON ON THE TOUCHLINE IN AUSTRALIA

The Chairman, who was Greek, wanted Greek players. I wanted English. Shortly after, I saw him going round collecting signatures at a match. I asked him what it was for and he told me it was a petition for my resignation. I said, 'Bring it over here and I'll sign it myself.'

Soon after I was on my way back to England and Preston North End. Unfortunately I was sacked after four months. So back I went to Australia. I spent more time in the Australian skies than the Flying Doctor.

I did six months with South Melbourne. Acutally, it should have been nine months but the Chairman gave me 3 months off for good behaviour.

From there I went to Wolves, via Sydney Olympic. At an early press conference a reporter said, 'I believe you intend doing for Wolves what J. F. Kennedy did for America,' It then occurred to me that John F. Kennedy got shot!

The end of my managerial career came at Altrincham, a non-league club in Cheshire. Which just goes to prove that money isn't everything.

MY ARRIVAL AT ALTRINCHAM

'What do you mean, "The Groundsman could do with a new hut?" That's your office!'

Even though the club was small I enjoyed my stay there. Of course, you couldn't compare it with Old Trafford or Hampden Park. To begin with, there was no clock in the ground, but I always knew when it was nearing half time because the players would start edging their way over to the dugout.

The players were keen enough but fitness was always a problem. I knew our right back wasn't good enough when I saw him going on an overlap at twenty past three and he made his way back at twenty past four. So I tried to inject some new blood. In fact, I signed so many new players that at the end of my pre-match pep talk I'd say, 'Right lads . . . best of luck, whoever you are.'

That almost brings us up to date. I left Altrincham in 1988, the Chairman followed soon after. I've no immediate plans regarding a return to football. In fact, the doctor told me to stay as far as I can from the game. So I might apply for the Manchester City job if it becomes vacant.

But just to highlight the insecurity of football management, I've included a few press cuttings. Throughout my stormy career I've collected quite a few. Some I'd prefer to forget. Whatever they say, right or wrong, it just goes to prove that you can't believe everything you read in the papers.

(SEE CENTRE PAGES)

That's all I'm going to say about the game. Well, almost all. I must tell you one story which epitomises all football chairmen. I won't name the man, but it involves the time he offered me a lift home. We left the club and walked to his Rolls Royce. I got in the passenger side and he took the seat behind the wheel. I was astonished when he picked up the evening paper and began to read it. After a couple of minutes I said, 'Mr Chairman. Hadn't you better start the car? We'll be here all night.' His answer was even more astonishing, although understandable. He slowly lowered the paper, looked at me and said, 'Sorry Tom, I thought YOU were driving!'

Now sit back and let me tell you about the other side of my life. As an after dinner speaker.

DINNERS IN GENERAL

To quote the words of an old comtemporary of mine, ' Speeches are funny old things '. There is no more satisfying sound than applause ringing in your ears after delivering a successful speech. But it's not quite that easy.

If Mark Twain had been on the present speech circuit I'm sure he would have been quoted as saying, ' The best way to spoil an excellent meal is to be a guest speaker. ' For nerves also play a big part.

Different speakers have different methods of overcoming their nerves. No two speakers are ever the same, although many of their jokes are! Some try beforehand to make their mind a complete blank, which isn't difficult if you're a football chairman. But if you don't experience a few nerves you'll never make a good speaker. Having said that, nerves can produce some horrific effects.

One speaker failed to conquer his nerves during a top business seminar and was so consumed by terror, he opted for the ultimate way out. He took the platform and turned to see five hundred people eagerly awaiting his address. This was all too much. He collapsed to the floor in a pretend faint and was hastily dragged off. The audience had no idea he was faking and showed the usual concern and sympathy. Unfortunately for the man, a business rival put it round that it was due to drink and the poor bloke was never invited back again.

Another question asked is why do it? The answer is manyfold. To some people it provides an opportunity to put over a point or message. To others, they can express themselves and entertain by way of a performance. I do it for the best reason of all. I get paid!

I've known speakers who charged fees so high that you'd need a crowd big enough to fill Wembley just to break even. Others do it for a nominal fee and a free dinner. What ever you pay as an organiser, the important thing is to get your money's worth.

A certain well known cricketer I know was invited to business dinner. I'm not a cricket fan, but I'm sure there were enough people interested in what he had to say. The delegates had spent three days intensive training on interview techniques, the majority of time being spent interviewing and questioning prospective job applicants. At the end of asking questions for three days they sat down to a nice meal, eagerly awaiting their guest's amusing after dinner speech. The guest stood up, introduced himself and said: ' I'm not a great speaker so what I'd like to do tonight is take questions from the audience! ' The response wasn't surprising. Needless to say he didn't receive a single question and left wondering what the hell he'd done to offend them. If you're a speaker you've got to give your money's worth.

'Trouble is, we've got to sell four million tickets just to break even.'

RECIPE FOR TOP TABLE DISASTER

The choice of top table guests can be difficult, but the rewards are great. The success of your dinner will be determined by the VIPs you invite.

If, for example, a sporting club intends raising money, then the correct choice of guests is of paramount importance. The more "Star Guests" you invite, the more tickets you'll sell.

But there are pitfalls. Say you invite a Sporting Star with a reputation for not turning up but you also know his name will generate interest. My advice to overcome this is simple. Invite him by all means, you'll have a sell out, but safeguard yourself by running a book. Advertise the attendance of the personality then give odds on him not turning up!

The next step is to strike a deal with the celebrity himself. Place a bet of a hundred pounds at 10-1 and offer him a cut if he actually turns up. This will ensure he does, and that you both make money. In fact, it might even be enough to cover your bail.

But what if he doesn't show up? I hear you ask. This is where some pre-planning is required. Have yourself a cheap standby speaker, someone who'd be lucky to sell twenty tickets. The money you save on the "Star's" fee will easily pay off the bets and the standby guest will only cost a fraction of that sum. Play on the punters sympathy. Say that your speaker has agreed to do the job at a minutes notice. They'll be so pleased with their winnings that any thought of a ticket refund will soon disappear.

RECIPE FOR TOP TABLE DISASTER

ADVICE ON VIP GUESTS

If a celebrity guest is required, go for a footballer. There are three reasons for this.

1. There are more of them.
2. They're cheaper.
3. You know the speech will be good because you've heard the same one from your last football speaker.

If you want a sell out, go for someone in the news. One way to ensure maximum publicity is to choose a well known name, then ring up a Sunday newspaper a couple of weeks before the event and say he's been seen at a drink and sex party. Don't worry about supplying evidence, never in my entire career have I known a Sunday tabloid to check out its facts.

'I've taken the liberty of arranging a couple of photographs, Brian.'

GREAT FOOD DISASTERS

A dinner menu has never sold tickets, unless you intend pre-announcing smoked salmon, caviar and champagne. Usually, the menu is a mystery until the guests arrive. In some cases it remains a mystery even after you've left!

I've had good and bad meals at Dinners. Some were so bad they should have been condemned by the council. Others were worthy of a SIX star hotel! But, wherever you are, whichever part of the country you're appearing in, you must adapt to local taste.

Up in the North West they have ' Lancashire Nights '. These usually involve a starter course of pigs feet, tripe, cow heels, or anything else the butcher wanted to throw out. Followed by steak and kidney pie, blackpuddings, potatoes etc. This is where the real north-south divide shows itself, I believe Jimmy Hill went to a dinner up in Lancashire and took an interpreter with him!

What was the worst meal I've ever had? I think it's got to be a local dish served up in Iraq. This time I wasn't speaking, but touring with a football club. We accepted the hospitality of our hosts and eagerly sat cross-legged on the floor. The opposing team sat opposite, chattering away and giving the odd smile. A huge gong was sounded and in walked a stream of waiters, six of whom were carrying a large metal dish. When the dish was lowered to the floor we couldn't believe our eyes. Perhaps that's the wrong choice of words. We couldn't believe THEIR eyes. For the plate was full of just that. Sheep's eyes! We sat in silence as the locals eagerly tucked in. The mood was eventually lightened by one of our players asking if there were enough to see us through the week.

'Is it my imagination or did that one on the end just wink?.'

Actually, one of our players did manage a couple of eyes. By the next morning I'd never seen him looking so ill, I hastily summoned the trainer who examined the player concerned. We decided that the only thing to do was to clear him out by using a suppository. He told the player to lie on his stomach and was about to insert the thing when he saw what seemed like an eye peering from the players bum! To which he said: ' Come on now Brian, we must learn to trust each other. '

Also, great care must be taken over the choice of food. There was a showbiz dinner attended by a large section of Jewish theatricals. The catering manager was mystified as to why two-thirds of the guests had declined the main meat course. He thought perhaps they were all vegetarians. Maybe the meat wasn't cooked. It never occurred to him that his choice of roast pork and bacon rolls might be responsible.

One thing does worry me though. It involves all the chickens which end up on our dinner table. I mean, every other function I attend has chicken on the menu. Sometimes every function! Chicken is a favourite with the organiser because it's plentiful and cheap! But I don't know if anyone's given any thought to what will happen if sportsmen's dinners become unpopular! Can you imagine all these birds suddenly set free? We'd have a country swarming with chickens!

'If only we hadn't ordered the food.'

Talking of that, I see MFI have merged with Sainsbury's. I realised when I bought a chicken and one of the legs were missing!

As for my own food preference, I have simple tastes, caviar, smoked salmon, a bottle of finest Chablis and a magnum of champagne. When I say simple taste, it's simple if you're sat next to Ron Atkinson at breakfast.

'ACKO' AT BREAKFAST

AUDIENCES

As well as the speaker, the audience is also responsible for making the night. Being a modest man, I can honestly say that I've never known a bad audience. But there are those who have.

'Hit me again. I can still hear him.'

I knew of one speaker who received so much stick from the audience that a punter at the back actually stood up and threw a wine bottle at him. It unfortuntely missed him and hit a gentleman sat near the front. The gent collapsed under the table, then was heard to mutter: ' Hit me again, I can still hear him! '

WHAT MAKES A GOOD AUDIENCE

A difficult question to answer, as all audiences are different. The correct amount of alcohol intake helps, although an excess can prove disastrous. (SEE WHAT MAKES A BAD AUDIENCE)

Judging their sense of humour is also difficult, I mean, I can tell a good story in Manchester but a London audience wouldn't laugh. Besides the fact they can't hear me, their sense of humour is different.

CAPTIVE AUDIENCES

The venue also has some bearing on this matter. It depends if the audience can go home if they don't like you. In some places they can't. Like ' Her Majesty's Hotels '. The inmates are locked in for a start. They also believe anything is better than going to bed at 6 o'clock after watching ' Blue Peter '.

'Psst . . . the breakout's been brought forward to tonight. Pass it on.'

WHAT MAKES A BAD AUDIENCE

Usually 10 pints of bitter and three bottles of wine each.

MY FAVOURITE AUDIENCE

This one is easy to answer. It's the audience who know I'm great and laugh a lot.

WHAT MAKES A GOOD SPEAKER

Articulate, witty, charming, a few amusing stories, good delivery, timing, confidence, interesting lifestyle, varied career.

Makes you wonder what makes ME so popular!

There are some notable speakers around today and people often ask who my favourite is. Well, being around so many dinners, I naturally see almost all of them. But as for naming my favourites? If I did that it would surely offend those I didn't mention. But seeing as I've never been bothered about offending people anyway, here goes.

My favourite After Dinner speakers are Peter Parfitt, the ex-cricketer and wit. Peter tells many stories of old Fiery Fred Trueman (no mean speaker himself) and of the Gentlemen who once played the game. Did I say Gentlemen? After twenty minutes of Peter you surely get a different impression of the cricket.

Wilf McGuiness, ex-Busby Babe. Although Wilf has lost all his hair he still looks the same as he did thirty years ago. He looked fifty then! I've known Wilf for a long time. Long before he was appointed manager of Manchester United. In fact, I knew Wilf when he HAD hair . . . and Elton John DIDN'T.

I also think highly of other speakers such as Arnie Martin, David Lloyd and Billy Thompson. In fact, I like anyone who's not as funny as me!

I also have favourite comedians. The king himself, Bernard Manning. Despite reports to the contrary, Bernard does a lot for charity. Only last week he was over in Stockport closing down a Variety Club Sunshine Home.

Other funny men I admire are Micky Finn and Vince Earl. Two of the funniest men ever to come out of Liverpool. That's if you don't count Derek Hatton. Of course they're not the only men who make me laugh. But we'll talk about Peter Swales and Ken Bates later on.

WHAT MAKES A BAD SPEAKER

See (WHAT MAKES A BAD AUDIENCE).

I once sat next to a chap who spent the entire evening telling me what a good dinner speaker he was. I couldn't understand how he ever remembered his lines because throughout the meal he was drinking like there was no tomorrow. His drinking session carried on throughout my own speech. Eventually, I finished to a standing ovation, the night was in aid of haemhorrhoid sufferers, and I sat down. This chap then stood up, said: ' Ladies and Gentlemen . . . ' and collapsed across the table. I never did find out how good he was!

As for unfunny speakers. Some of the worst ones I've ever heard also happen to be the people with the biggest reputations.

Two of the biggest bores I've ever encountered are an ex-cricket captain and a chairman of a football club. In fact, they were to After Dinner Speaking what King Herod was to baby sitting.

Someone did tell me that Derek Dougan has embarked on an international career, boring for England, but I believe it only to be a rumour. But I'll say this for Derek, his speeches are always a test for your kidneys. Mind you, he has done wonders for road safety. Whenever you sit down to a Derek Dougan speech you can be sure of going home in the daylight.

EIGHT DIFFERENT WAYS TO GET PAID

1. Used notes in cash.
2. Unused notes in cash.
3. Cheque.
4. Access/Visa.
5. You scratch my back and I'll scratch yours.
6. Do this one free and I'll get you tons of work.
7. You need the publicity.
8. It's for a good cause. The orphans haven't had a holiday for years.

'Right, 500 cash. Give 'em a chance to dry before putting them in your wallet.'

ELEVEN EXCUSES FOR NOT BEING PAID

1. The cheque's in the post.
2. The treasurer's off ill.
3. We need another signature on the cheque.
4. We've sent it to your old address.
5. We thought we'd booked Brian Clough.
6. We've got a cash flow problem. (WHAT FOOTBALL CLUB DOESN'T?)
7. We haven't counted the raffle money yet.
8. The tickets haven't been paid for yet.
9. Go and see the Chairman. (NEVER TO BE FOUND)
10. The sponsor's pulled out.
11. The Secretary's on holiday in Marbella. (USUALLY WITH THE CLUB FUNDS)

AUTOGRAPHS

A large part of any 'Celebrity's' time is taken up with signing autographs. It is usual to spend half an hour or so signing menus after giving a speech. That's assuming the punter has a menu for you to sign.

I've had some unusual things to sign in my time. Ties, bald heads, bits of toilet paper, bus tickets, five pound notes, shirt tails. But the most unusual one was a ladies bra! She unashamedly removed it in full view, placed it on the table, and gave me a pen. I'm not saying she was a big woman, but I could have written the entire collection of War and Peace on one cup!

'Just sign it "Best wishes", Tom.'

I was once involved in a funny request. A woman gave me a piece of paper and said: 'Could you sign it for my son, Mr. Clough.'

I replied: 'But I'm Tommy Docherty!'

She said: 'That's alright. He can't read anyway.'

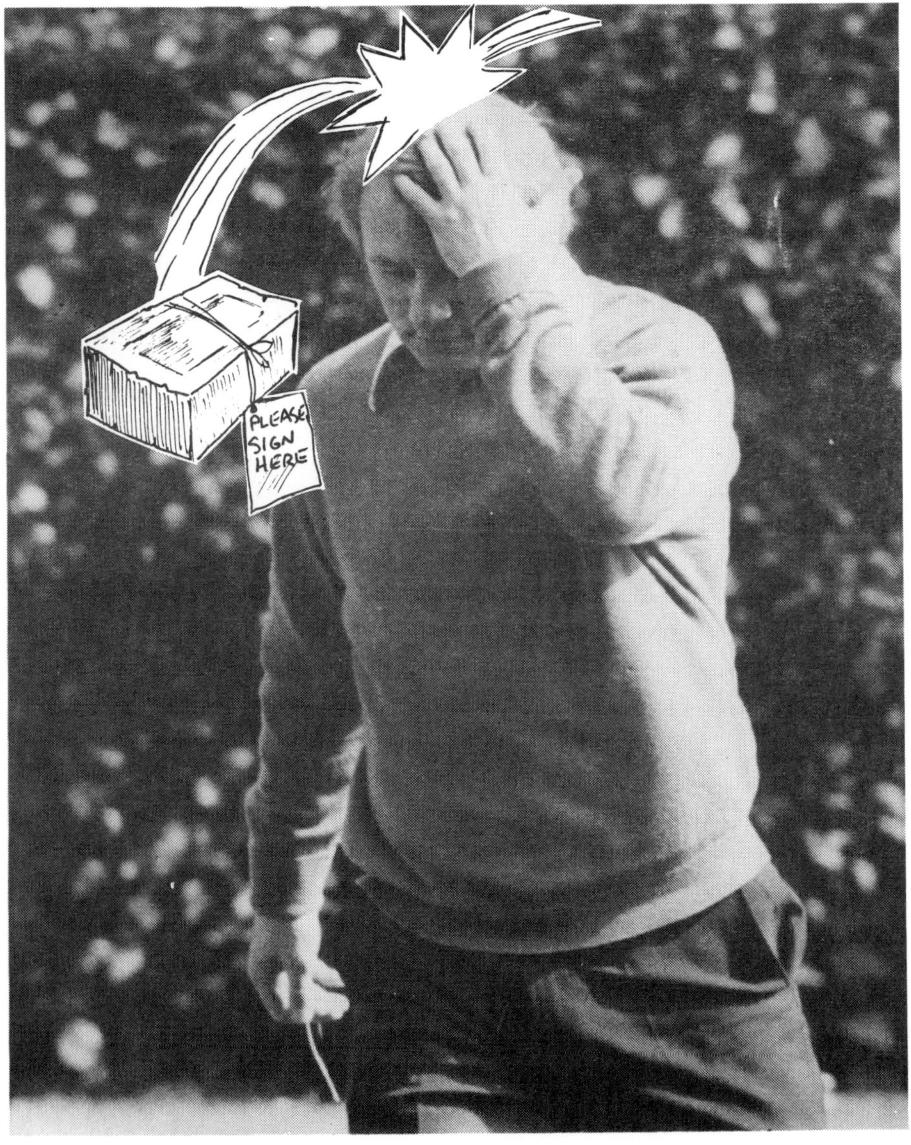

A USUAL REQUEST FOR MY AUTOGRAPH

THE FIRST STEP TOWARDS A SUCCESSFUL SPEAKING CAREER

BOXING DINNERS

Boxing dinners provide the exception to the rule. Not only are you required to speak, but have to do it from the ring!

I know of one sportsman who was approached for a boxing night. It was explained that he would be speaking from the ring to which he said: ' Isn't that a bit dangerous? I could get hurt! '

So my advice to any boxing night organiser is to put the speaker in AFTER the boxing's finished.

MY EXPERIENCES AT DINNERS

For many after dinner speakers, travel is a necessary evil. To be in Southampton one night and Newcastle the next is commonplace. The half an hour a punter sees you on your feet is just the tip of the iceberg. What he doesn't see is the countless hours spent behind a steering wheel driving to and from the event. As most dinners occur during the winter months, most of that time is spent driving through fog, ice and snow!

Boredom is also a problem. Driving a four hundred mile round trip is like watching ninety minutes of Manchester City. It's that bad! So how do you relieve the boredom? Having someone to talk to helps, but it's not advisable to pick up a hitchiker these days. In fact, I've only ever picked up a hitchiker once, and only then because it was me who knocked him over. I've found the best method is to have a good laugh. So now I just play an old tape I've had for years, 'Peter Swales on football'.

I remember one day in particular. It was late January and light flurries of snow were falling on the lawn outside. I was enjoying a mug of coffee by an open fire and asked my wife, Mary, what was in our diary for the next evening. She looked and calmly announced it was Sunderland. The snow began to resemble a blizzard, Sunderland seemed even further away. I recalled my previous drive there being the worst of my life. And that was in August! It was obvious I'd need to leave early, so next day I set off resembling John Mills in 'Scott of the Antarctic'.

It took me seven hours of crawling, slithering and sliding. At one stage I was stuck in a drift when a helpful police car stopped. The two officers turned out to be the only Manchester United supporters in the North East so I gratefully accepted their offer of a tow. Eventually we arrived at the venue, a social club who's name I've long since forgotten. Was I glad to see the organiser waiting at the door. I signed autographs for the patrolmen and invited them inside for a drink. Being on duty they accepted. The organiser gave me a welcome typical of the North East saying, 'Tommy, good to see you bonny lad!' I explained it was due to a little help from my friends the local police and he replied, 'The main thing is you've made it.' Then added, 'It's a pity the audience didn't!'

It transpired that the entire audience had been stuck in the same blizzard! There was only one thing I could do. I gave a speech to a grateful club secretary and two motorway policemen!

'If he comes out with that word again I'm nicking him for foul and abusive language.'

But there are speakers who go over the top. One bloke told a joke which required him to fire a gun when he gave the punchline. Unfortunately, he didn't know that the Chairman had a long standing heart complaint. He got to the end of his joke, took out a revolver and fired it. The speech did carry on, eventually, but only after the Chairman had been given cardiac massage and removed to hospital.

I've even known an explosives expert to light a stick of dynamite, give it to a punter to hold and leave the room! He knew it to be a dummy, I knew it to be a dummy, even the punter holding it must have had his suspicions. Even so, it worked wonders on my bowel movements so goodness knows what it did to the poor soul holding ten pounds of TNT with sweat running down his face.

'Of course it's a dummy! But just in case it's not we're off home.'

IRISH DINNERS

Dinner to an Englishman is tradition. From the arrival of the top table guest, to the exit of the Port, like it or not, the English are great organisers. Makes you wonder how they lost the European Championships. Every function follows the same pattern of reception, soup, meal, sweet, port, coffee and mints, after dinner speech, vote of thanks, then off home. That's in England.

But things are different in Ireland. I've had some wonderful nights over there, sampling Irish hospitality and listening to their masterful understatements. Things like, 'Was it you or dat other player who was killed in the plane crash, Tom?'

One English tradition is definitely out in the staunch Republican areas. Let me explain. I was booked to give a speech at Cork Football Club alongside a very funny Irish comic called Dusty Young. The M.C. for the night was Alan Platt, a man well versed in procedure. The punters were finishing their sweet when Alan was heard to remark, 'Looks like they could do with a smoke.' He then stood up and filled his glass. Dusty was horrified and whispered to me, 'I hope he's not doing what I think he's doing!' It then occurred to me what Dusty meant. Out of habit, our M.C. was about to give the Loyal Toast. At the point of 'Gentlemen please be upstanding . . .' Dusty grabbed the microphone and quickly added, 'Those of you who'd like to go out for a pee, that is!'

Goodness knows how the Irish would have reacted to, 'The Queen'! As it was, we saved the night, and our necks in the process.

This also could only happen in Ireland. That particular dinner was the first arranged for a Monday. Unfortunately, on the Saturday before, I had to cancel and asked for the event to be re-arranged. I received a call saying they were holding it on Tuesday instead. I enquired which Tuesday? They told me, 'Next Tuesday'. It then struck me that 400 people had bought tickets, it must be virtually impossible to contact them all! 'But it's now Sunday!' I said. The reply didn't surprise me. 'Don't worry Mr Docherty, sir. We'll see they get to know.'

I am now convinced that everybody in Ireland had everybody else's phone number. Because I turned up to a packed house!

Jack Charlton also had a memorable experience at Cork. He was well into his speech when a top table guest asked for more coffee. A little Irish waiter was summoned and began making his way along the line pouring out cups. He came to Jack, who was by now in the middle of a story about playing for England. The waiter tapped him on the shoulder. The conversation went like this . . .

JACK: Which reminds me of a World Cup game in 1966 . . .

WAITER: Excuse me Mr Charlton. Would you be wanting coffee?

JACK: Coffee? Err, yes. (to audience) I was lined up facing a free.

WAITER: Would you be wanting milk, sir?

JACK: No, black will do. (to audience) Our Bobby was in the wall next to me. Now, Bobby could take free kicks but didn't like facing them . . .

WAITER: Sugar, Mr Charlton?

JACK: No sugar. (To audience) So I told Bobby, don't move.

WAITER: Right sir. I won't bother you again. If you want anything else just give me a nod. I'll be over there.

The waiter then left, unaware that he'd been responsible for interrupting Jack Charlton's best story.

I have experienced Irish nights in England. That's where the entire evening is organised backwards. You have the speech, followed by coffee, sweet, main course and soup. In that order! It was different if nothing else. And believe me — it's also true!

I've also experienced some unusual methods of payment. I think the most unusual was up in the far north of England. It was a charity do for some local society. The organiser, seeing as there was no fee involved, decided he must reimburse my expenses. So at the end of the night I was proudly presented with two pheasants and bottle of English wine. Goodness knows what that would look like on the tax returns.

'I thought you'd like to take your 33 percent before we have dinner.'

SPEECH MATERIAL

It's obvious that a speaker's material must suit his audience. Having said that, I've known many a speaker who's died a death solely due to the wrong choice of material. Unless you have a national reputation for a strong act, such as Bernard Manning, my advice is to stay clear of the blue stuff.

Having said that, there was a time when I failed to get through to one certain member of the audience. A time when I began to doubt my own speech content.

The speech was well received. Everyone was laughing in the right places, almost everyone that is. One particular man, who was sat near the front, remained stone faced throughout the first fifteen minutes. I knew he couldn't be deaf because I'd seen him conversing with the man next to him. On reaching my best story I thought, 'Right. He's got to laugh at this one.' I ended to thunderous applause but the old chap just sat there without a flicker! By this time I had begun to question myself, I rounded off with a few quick gags and sat down. Despite the congratulations, all I could think about was this miserable so and so at the front. So I put it to the organiser. Was he just plain miserable? 'No,' replied the organiser, 'He's just a German who can't speak a word of English!'

One advantage of being the main guest is that you can be sure of a warm welcome from the audience. But my sympathy goes out to the supporting comics. To stand up at twelve minutes to midnight when ninety percent of the audience are worse for drink is no joke! At this stage your material becomes IMMATERIAL! But if the night is young and the audience are in a position to respond, then you've got to watch it.

The most common 'cock up' is the innocent, unintentional remark. Remarks like, 'The Chairman's wife is so big that she has to move off the beach before the tide can come in!' This was once compounded by the fact that the Chairman's wife had actually been drowned the week before! Believe me, I witnessed a comic make that mistake!

'Which reminds me of the story about the Scotsman, the Arab and the Jew!'

Another common mistake is a reference to the wrong team. Remember that places like Liverpool and Manchester have TWO teams each! Also that supporters do not wear their colours to a dinner.

I made that mistake when I was speaking at a Rugby dinner in the North West and queried a gag with the M.C. I enquired who the most unpopular team was in those parts and was told it was Widnes. I got to the punchline and gave it, unaware that the club I was appearing at was in a suburb of Widnes. The only laughter came from the M.C., who thought the fact that I'd just insulted ninety percent of the audience was hilarious.

Docherty faces his third vote of confidence

By ALAN WILLIAMS

TOMMY DOCHERTY, manager of bottom-the-Second-Division ...n Villa, faces ano... board meet... k to...

Doug Ellis ... City

DON'T BELIEVE EVERYTHING YOU READ IN THE PAPERS

Villa meeting: Docherty is 'confident'

by DENNIS SHAW

...my Docherty ...

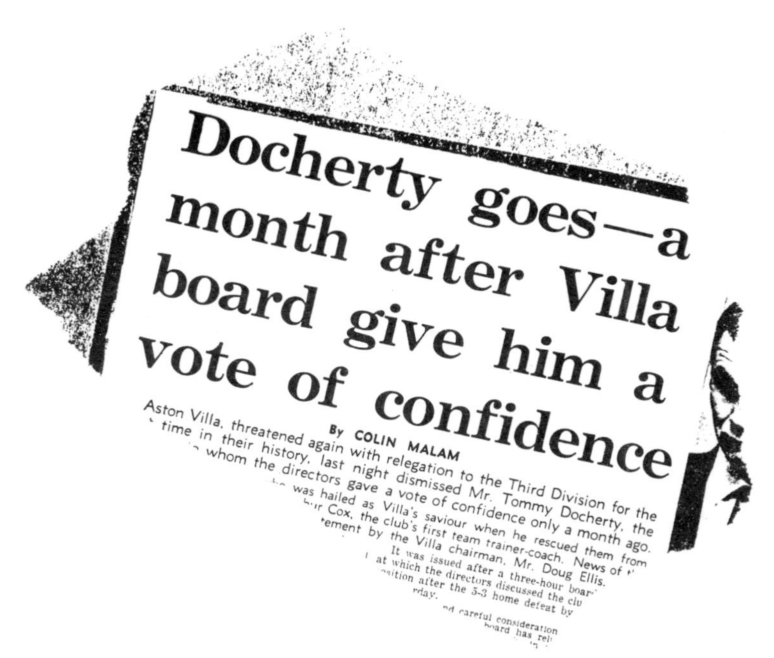

Docherty goes—a month after Villa board give him a vote of confidence

By COLIN MALAM

Aston Villa, threatened again with relegation to the Third Division for the … time in their history, last night dismissed Mr. Tommy Docherty, the … whom the directors gave a vote of confidence only a month ago. … was hailed as Villa's saviour when he rescued them from … Cox, the club's first team trainer-coach. News of … statement by the Villa chairman, Mr. Doug Ellis. It was issued after a three-hour board … at which the directors discussed the club … position after the 5-3 home defeat by … day.

… careful consideration … board has …

DON'T BELIEVE EVERYTHING YOU READ IN THE PAPERS

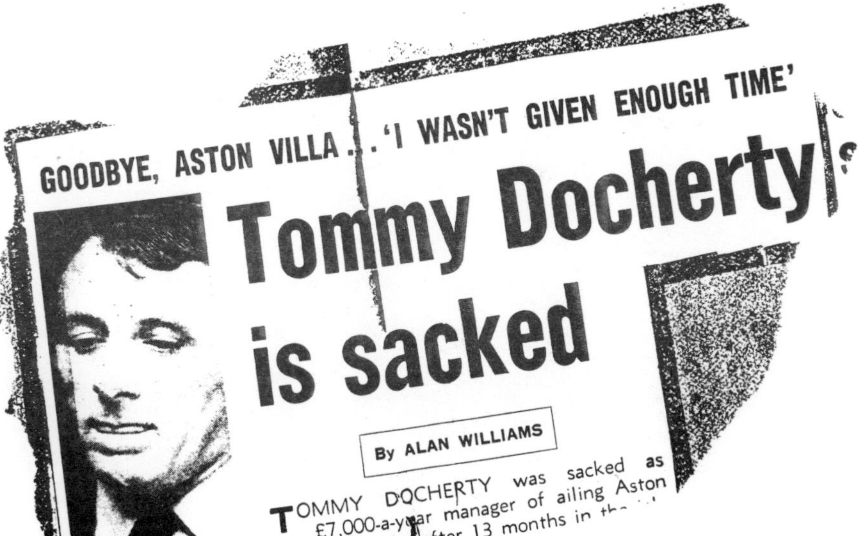

GOODBYE, ASTON VILLA . . . 'I WASN'T GIVEN ENOUGH TIME'

Tommy Docherty is sacked

By ALAN WILLIAMS

TOMMY DOCHERTY was sacked as £7,000-a-year manager of ailing Aston Villa last night after 13 months in the …

Only three weeks ago he … confidence" from the boar…

DOCHERTY LAST NIGHT

AFTER BEING TOLD OF MY APPOINTMENT AS MANAGER OF ALTRINCHAM

AFTER BEING GIVEN THE SACK BY ALTRINCHAM

TOMMY DOCHERTY PICTURED WITH THE BOARD OF DIRECTORS AT WOLVES

A RARE PICTURE. THE ONLY TIME GEORGE TURNED UP FOR TRAINING

SPEAKING ABROAD

Sometimes the opportunity comes along to widen your horizons and speak abroad. One of the most desirable and popular places I know of is Monte Carlo.

Numerous businessmen elect to hold their meetings and seminars in Monte, so it follows that a speaker must travel there to entertain. One secret for a speaker is to stay out of the Casinos and actually come back with more money than you went out with. Most heed this advice, a few don't. I know of one certain sportsman who was paid a fee of £1,000 but came back £1,500 out of pocket. As for me? I'm a Scot, so I've never experienced any trouble.

Another popular venue is the 'Costa Del Crime' on Spain's southern coast. The residents are often homesick, with a home that's impossible to return to, so a few home comforts are shipped over instead. And I've never met a more appreciative audience.

They usually take place on a stretch of coast between Estapona and Marbella. A route lined with million dollar mansions and affluent apartment blocks. This also takes in a little fishing port called Puerto Banus, where the local quay is lined with ocean going yachts, big enough to put the Fred Olsen line to shame!

When the natives become restless for some entertainment the call goes out. 'Organise a sportsman's dinner'.

I was invited over to Marbella recently as guest speaker. Actually, they had a choice of me or John Stalker but I think John was off on one of his Murder Weekends up in the Lake District. In fact, had he accepted the Marbella job he could investigated a few real ones!

I flew over by private charter plane. I'm not saying it was old but you could see where the swastikas had been painted out on the wings.

I was met at the airport by a black Mercedes, who's driver was similarly attired. It seems that my chauffeur was a Manchester lad who dearly missed the football at Maine Road. I had to point out that over the past few years we ALL missed the football at Maine Road. He drove me from the airport to Marbella along the famous highway of death. We only stopped twice. Once for petrol and once for me to change my trousers.

We arrived at the hotel, the best on the coast, and I went for a lie down to recuperate from my journey.

At 6 p.m. prompt I was awakened by a loud banging on the bedroom door. I opened it to find my chauffeur. I also noticed the occupants of the adjacent rooms making for the fire escape. It seems that a loud banging of any door has that effect on certain people over there.

When I arrived at the venue the VIP list was like a script from 'Police Five'! All the big names were there. Anyone who is anyone on the Costa Del Crime. And if you think I'm naming names you've got to be joking! I intend to enjoy some of the profit from this book. After shaking hands with the top table guests, with a brief pause to count my fingers afterwards, something suddenly struck me. No, it wasn't a knuckle duster, but the fact that I was the only one present who could legally return to England after it was over. And that included the women!

I did my speech, brilliant as ever, and the raffle was conducted. The third prize was a gold medallion. The second prize was two dozen Rolex watches. But what a first prize! Something everyone present would like to get their hands on. A used UK passport!

A TYPICAL M.C. ON THE COSTA DEL CRIME!

RAFFLES AND AUCTIONS

Raffles and auctions are good earners for big and small clubs alike.

Anything can be auctioned, and often is, from a well known player's underpants to a book signed by a famous World War Two fighter pilot. There's only one criteria, there must be somebody willing to bid.

An auction took place up in the North East, involving an autographed football. The M.C. started off the bidding at five pounds. It quickly increased to twenty, with a particular punter intent on buying. The M.C. said, 'Twenty five, who'll give me twenty five pounds?' Up went the punters hand. 'Thirty . . . anyone give me thirty?' A voice from the back shouted, yes. 'Thirty five? Thirty five pounds.' The punter sensing the opposition, jumped to his feet and shouted 'Thirty seven pounds, forty eight pence!' An odd figure, I thought.

'Going once, going twice . . . sold!

The ball was removed and the punter came over to collect it. The M.C. was also puzzled at this particular bid. 'Tell me, son, why thirty seven pounds, forty eight pence?'

The lad took out a slip of paper and replied, 'Cause that's what's on my Giro cheque!'

This poor lad was actually paying for the ball with his unemployment benefit.

'I'd have bought the autographed football as well if my invalidity benefit hadn't just been stopped.'

Then there was the raffle where the organiser sold fifteen books of tickets. There was only one problem, he sold both halves of the book and put different numbers in the drum. After the guest of honour had drawn out twenty three tickets without a single winner the audience became suspicious. The organiser became distraught after realising what he'd done. It was close to midnight when the draw was made and he was faced with the problem of how to give the money back! They resolved the matter by the guest shutting his eyes and flinging beer mats at the audience. Whoever it hit won a prize! Which was a simple, if not unorthodox method of choosing a winner!

'We've unfortunately lost the raffle tickets. So to determine the winner of tonight's star prize . . .'

My favourite auctions occur during testimonial dinners. I'm often amazed at the rubbish that's sold off in aid of a player. Don't get me wrong, I'm not against any player making a few bob at the end of his career, but to sell off items that wouldn't fetch two pence at a jumble sale is going too far.

Let me explain. If you went to a shop and they offered a cream pullover, full of holes and smelling of linement, for eighty pounds, what would you say? Probably the same as me, 'Stuff it!'

But what if it belonged to an international cricketer? Would you pay that amount then? Believe me, plenty of punters do. So many that I now travel about in a car full of Docherty old ties and socks in the hope that one day an entrepeneur will snap them up.

Another con is the testimonial year official programme. To me, a programme is something to use before and during an event. Why do you need one afterwards? A question I've often asked because that's when they go on sale. You've already heard what the bloke had to say, and the night's over so the order of events is no use to you. The reason is simple. Souvenirs. So if anyone fancies an old Docherty tie, please write to the publisher who will supply one at a reasonable cost.

In fact, I did once have a tie which was auctioned. The organiser had sold off everything possible and asked if I'd donate the tie I was wearing. I naturally agreed and was amazed when a two pounds Marks and Sparks tie fetched twenty four quid!

I remember George Best outbidding himself for a piece of club memorabilia. It was during a charity dinner when George was going through his falling over spell. George was on vodka and windolene, it didn't taste very good but at least your eyes were clear the next morning.

The bidding started off at five pounds and quickly reached a hundred. George, oblivious to the other bidders, came in with a bid of a hundred and ten. It was accepted and any advance asked for. George shouted, 'A hundred and twenty!'. Accepted once again. Any more offers? 'A hundred and thirty five,' replied George. He eventually got the piece for a hundred and fifty pounds. To which the organiser thanked George and reminded him that he'd just been responsible for the last six bids!

One night I even found myself caught up in the proceedings. A diamond ring was being auctioned off and I thought, as guest of honour, I should make a bid myself. I shouted out, 'Three hundred and fifty!' To my horror, the room fell silent. I was then mortified by the following words, 'Sold to Mr Docherty for three hundred and fifty pounds.' I took the ring home as a present to my wife. The next week, just out of interest, she had it valued. It turned out to be worth a hundred and ninety five pounds. Ah well, some you win and some you get done over.

Believe it or not, the most bizarre auction involved a plate of cheese and biscuits. The audience had been whipped into a frenzy as bids went through the roof. The M.C. had absolutely nothing left to sell. He leaned across and asked me for my plate of cheese and biscuits. I was amazed at the outcome. They went for seven pounds!

PEOPLE AS SPEAKERS

POLITICIANS: On the whole, are confident speakers. Let's face it, anyone who can get away with talking for three hours without saying anything must be confident! The most common political figures on the sporting circuit are the Ministers for Sport. I've heard some good ones as well as bad, but they've all got one thing in common. They enjoy the sound of their own voice.

I know Cyril Smith does a bit of speaking but you've got to be careful who you sit him next to. Not because he's fussy, but because when Cyril's at the top table there's no room for anyone else! And if big Cyril and Bernard Manning ever appear on the same bill they'll have to build an extension to the club!

Nobody actually eats in there. It's for Big Cyril and Bernard to change in.'

POLICEMEN

There are one or two policemen making a name for themselves on the circuit. You'd be surprised how funny they can be, even if their subject matter verges on the gruesome side. I know of two ex-murder squad officers who now give speeches on that subject. One talks about a series of chilling murders and the other . . . well, the other does the same I suppose.

When I first heard them I thought, 'How the hell can they make a joke out of this?' But they succeeded. That's the secret of a good speaker. Never offend. Mind you, I did notice one or two of the more sensitive types leaving to take some fresh air. Of course, to their friends, they were going to the toilet for a pee. But we all know the real reason.

'And then there was the case of the severed arm!'

FOOTBALLERS

Footballers, I know about. Many ex-footballers turned managers are presently speaking. In my view, football managers fall into the following categories.

Football Managers

Ex Football Managers

People who think they are Football Managers

People who wish they were Football Managers

People who could never be Football Managers

International Managers fall into two groups

Successful Managers

Unsuccessful Managers

CRICKETERS

Cricketers are a breed unto themselves. Some are ex-Public Schoolboys who have as much in common with the average audience as the Ayotollah Khomene does! Others are lads from ordinary backgrounds who've made a name for themselves swinging a piece of wood.

Whatever their background, the subject matter is always the same. The story of Fiery Freddie Trueman taking on the West Indies. What's Ian Botham like on and off . . . the field that is. The secret behind Mike Gatting oversleeping in Australia. Even I know that one! The reason was as follows: the trainer set the alarm clock for eleven but only ten of them got up!

THE CLERGY

In my experience, clergymen make excellent speakers. A number of Bishops are presently doing the circuit and astonishing audiences with their natural wit. On the subject of Bishops, I have one piece of advice. If you also have a comic on the bill put him on last. That way the Bishop can leave should he wish to do so.

'So these two Bishops go into a Brothel . . .'

GOLFING DINNERS

I don't personally play golf, although I'm often invited along to golfing dinners. There's only one trouble with a golf dinner, it's usually full of golfers eating, breathing and talking golf. Back nine holes and birdies are alien to me, almost like a foreign language. It always reminds me of football chairmen at board meetings. You know the game but haven't got a clue how to play it!

I did once play a round. Not play around as in professional footballers, but a round of golf. Unfortunately, the string broke after six hits and I lost the ball.

A favourite with the golfing fraternity is the 'Celebrity Match'. I use the word Celebrity in the loosest context of the word. For if I'd paid a hundred and fifty quid to partner a comic who's only claim to fame was being slagged off by Tony Hatch on New Faces in 1976 I think I'd demand a refund.

V.I.P.'s

Being the main guest has the advantage, or disadvantage if you like, of being classed as a V.I.P. This usually involves a reception before the dinner to meet the sponsors and organisers. It also involves the unnerving experience of being clapped to the table by the punters. When I say unnerving, it's because the handclap is traditionally a slow one! Fortunately, after forty years of football I'm well used to that.

But that's providing you're being clapped TO the table. I remember Wilf McGuinness saying to me that he found the slow handclap we were receiving quite amusing. He stopped laughing when I explained we were on our way OUT of the room!

Photographs are yet another obligatory part of being a V.I.P. Photographs with the organiser, the sponsor, the chairman, the chairman's wife, the chairman's dog, etc. I have never objected to posing for a photograph, unless you count the time I appeared at the Old Bailey, but I did object to one photographer charging five quid a picture. I felt even worse when I found out the punters were buying them to hang over the mantlepiece . . . to keep the kids away from the fire!

HECKLERS

One golden rule for speakers is not to leave yourself open to a funny remark made by a punter. Especially a remark that's funnier than yours!

If, for example, you aren't sure if the P.A. system is working, never ask, 'Can you hear me at the back?'. Because there's always someone who'll shout out, 'Yes, but I'll swap for someone who can't!'

An example of this happened when I appeared on the same bill as Lenny Bennett. The night was to be rounded off with a celebrity snooker match with Lenny partnering Steve Davis. But before this, we had the speeches. I finished mine to the usual ovation and Lenny followed. Unfortunately, what followed Lenny was silence. It wasn't one of his best performances.

We set off for the snooker room where Lenny fared a bit better. He was left with a black ball pot to win the game. He lined up his cue and muttered to Steve, 'If I miss this one I'll die.' To which a punter within earshot shouted out, 'That'll make it twice in one night then!'

Any comic worth his salt will experience little difficulty in putting down a heckler. But sportsmen aren't comics so the best method I've found is to ignore the remark, or even join in the fun. As I did myself after meeting my present wife, Mary. And those particular remarks came from the best people around. The Kop at Anfield!

9 ~~TEN~~ THINGS YOU DIDN'T KNOW ABOUT TOMMY DOCHERTY (OR TEN THINGS YOU COULDN'T CARE LESS ABOUT)

1. He's had ~~seventeen~~ clubs.
2. He's funny.
3. He's modest.
4. He's sincere.
5. He's generous.
6. He's human.
7. He's never had a Cup Final ticket since he was caught selling them.
8. He's the best after dinner speaker around.
9. He's the best value for money around.
10. HE TELLS LIES.

BOXERS

Again, not many about. The most notable ones being Jim Watt and Henry Cooper. Poor old 'Enery suffered cut eyes throughout his distinguished career. Which, in fact, affected his number of wins. If he hadn't cut so easily he could have been knocked out a lot more!

SNOOKER PLAYERS

Few and far between. John Virgo proving a notable exception. Who could forget his impressions of famous snooker players? Almost everyone who's seen him, I should think. Seriously though, John does the best snooker impressions around. Come to think of it, John does the ONLY snooker impressions around!

'I'll tell you how we can afford it! Mike Yarwood's doing the lot for five hundred.'

JUDGES

Judges always have something to say worth listening to. As I found out during my trial at the Old Bailey. I was asked how I pleaded and replied, 'Guilty.' The Judge said, 'I don't believe you.'

'One can always tell when Mr Docherty is lying. His lips move.'

CHIMNEY SWEEPS

Not many about. In fact, I only know of one. Fred Dibnah. Fred used to travel everywhere by steam roller. I believe one organiser refused to let him park it in the official car park. But Fred soon ironed out the problem. Together with the Committee's cars!

'Alright, which idiot told Fred Dibnah his speech was rubbish.'

DIVES I'VE WORKED IN

I've worked in many clubs over the years. Sporting, social, Round Table, you name it and I've appeared there. Most are pleasant, friendly places. Some are less friendly. I've experienced clubs in the North where the A Team wouldn't even go into for a drink. I've met club secretaries, who, when a speaker has mentioned he was the night's entertainment, the secretary has replied, 'Not yet, you're not.'

So below I've listed some of the dives I've actually worked in:

Chelsea	Coach 1961
	Manager 1962
Rotherham United	Manager 1967
Queens Park Rangers	Manager 1968
Aston Villa	Manager 1968
Oporto	Coach 1970
Hull City	Assistant Manager 1971
Scotland	Caretaker Manager 1971
	Manager 1971
Manchester United	Manager 1972
Derby County	Manager 1977
Queens Park Rangers	Manager 1979
Sydney Olympic	Coach 1980
Preston North End	Manager 1981
South Melbourne	Coach 1981
Sydney Olympic	Coach 1982
Wolverhampton Wanderers	Manager 1983
Altrincham	Manager 1987
Stringfellows	Customer 1988
Browns	Customer 1988
Wigmore Street	Consultant, Awaiting Acceptance

THE DOC'S A TO Z OF DINNERS

A QUICK REFERENCE DICTIONARY OF SPEAKERS AND SPEAKING

A

AFTER DINNER SPEAKER: Male or female with slight masochistic tendencies. Extrovert. Must be willing to stand on feet for at least 30 minutes, sometimes to complete silence. Also, must be conversant with counting 20 pound notes in the toilet.

AFTER DINNER SPEECH: A string of stories given by an after dinner speaker. Sometimes original, most stolen from other speakers. Content ranges from the blue to the boring.

AUDIENCE: Vary in size, sometimes like piles. Come in large groups and are a pain in the backside.

B

BOOZE, BIRDS, BED, BONKING, BEST G., BOTHAM I.

BAN: Experienced by many after dinner speakers whilst attempting to drive home.

C

CLUB: Venue for after dinner speeches. Usually with sporting connections, with the exception of Manchester City.

CELEBRITY: Usually an ex-sportsman after a free meal but won't pay the price of a ticket.

CATASTROPHY, CLOUGH, CROKER (see what makes a bad speaker), CRICKET, CAPTAIN, CRUMPET.

D

DINNER: A meal never enjoyed by an after dinner speaker.

DOC: (See what makes a good speaker)

DOUGAN D: Puts more people to sleep than my dentist.

DRINK, DRIVING (Occupational Hazard) (see ban)

E

ENVELOPE: Recepticle for transporting a fee to a speaker. Usually plain. Can be white or brown. These must be opened out of sight of organiser before speaker leaves to ensure he hasn't been done! (See toilet)

F

FORUM: Lame excuse for a celebrity taking questions from the floor because he's incapable of giving a speech.

FUTURE: Desirable commodity for after dinner speakers. Alien to most football managers.

G

GAGS: Material used by speakers. Can be bought from scriptwriter but more commonly stolen from each other.
GASP: A noise coming from an audience when a joke misfires. (See M for McGuinness)

H

HOTELS: Popular venues for after dinner speeches. Also place of pre-match training for English cricketers.

I

INSTITUTION: As in Bernard Manning. Or where he should possibly be.

I . . I . . I can't think of anything else.

J

JUMPERS: Often sold off at inflated prices by cricketers at testimonial dinners.

JUDGES. JOCKSTRAPS: Both responsible for keeping sportsmen in nick!

K

KITTY: Common method of payment for group of drinkers. Or money shared out between players at end of season.

KAT: Spelling was never a Docherty strong point.

L

LIVERPOOL. CITY OF: Unusual travel arrangements here of driving to venue and walking home.

LIVERPOOL F.C. LEAGUE: Looks likely.

M

M.C.: Master of Ceremonies. Usually a comic who can't get any other work.

N

NOVEMBER: Popular time for dinners. Also for Liverpool F.C. tying up the League.

O

OCTOBER: Same as November if Liverpool F.C. have a good run.

OVERNIGHT ACCOMMODATION: Shelter for weary speakers. Especially welcome when reaching the falling over stage of a night.

P

PEE BREAK: A ten minute break given to an audience before the speaker stands up. This ensures that no one leaves the room in mid-story.

PUNTER: The people who matter. Without their money there wouldn't be any dinner scene.

Q

QUESTIONS: Sometimes coupled with answers. They come in sessions. Usually when a celebrity has no talent for speaking.

R

RAFFLE: A form of lottery ensuring revenue for the organisers. Usually tickets are drawn by the guest. Prizes range from hip flasks to autographed footballs and club ties. Club ties are always the last prize to be claimed.

READIES: Popular method of payment. (See E for Envelope).

RECEIPT: Required by speaker to sign before payment. Usually with someone else's name.

RELIEF: Experienced by audiences at the end of Derek Dougan's speech.

REBUFF: When Derek Dougan was asked his opinion of Tommy Docherty.

S

SCANDAL: Tactics of Manchester City. Content of Docherty's speech.

SAINT & GREAVSIE: Who did for after dinner speaking what Cyril Smith and Bernard Manning did for synchronised swimming.

T

TOILET: Place for counting money received in plain envelope.

TRASH, TROUBLE, TRUEMAN: Subject of all cricketers speeches.

TAYLOR G. PFA SECRETARY: Also after dinner speaker. Or so he tells us.

U

UNITED, MANCHESTER, UNEMPLOYED: (See D for Doc).

V

VENUE: Place for holding dinner.

VELCOME: Received at Jewish dinners.

W

WELCOME: Received at Christian dinners.

X

XYLOPHONE: Not often played at dinners but nothing else I know begins with X.

Y

Y BOTHER!: As muttered by many organisers.

Z

ZULUS: Don't often make good audiences.

Nick Owen

Nick Owen started off in life as a journalist. Since then he has become a familiar face on TV.

I first met Tommy Docherty when he was manager of Derby County and I was reporting for Central TV. As usual, Tommy was always available for comment.

Then we worked together on TV AM, where I was the presenter and Tommy a regular guest. Whenever he appeared you could count on one thing, he was sure to brighten up the morning. Not only for viewers but for the crew as well. Many a time he's reduced the cameramen to tears. Sometimes he reduced the director to tears, but only because he wouldn't sit still long enough to stay in focus.

The main thing I remember is the laughs we shared. Now he's gone on to be an author, but one thing has disappointed me about the book. He didn't have time to colour the cartoons in. Still, now that he's out of football he can spend those long winter nights by his fire colouring them in.

Wilf McGuiness

Ex-Busby Babe, ex-manager of Manchester United, presently coach and physio to Bury F.C. and prominent after dinner speaker.

When I was approached by the co-author for this article, he said he wanted to interview some people who'd worked with the Doc. I told him he'd have more difficulty finding someone who HASN'T worked with the Doc!

What can I say about Tommy Docherty which hasn't already been quoted by the press. Not much, except for my own personal view.

The Doc has helped me enormously over the years. On one particular occasion, I was returning from Greece at a time when the Doc was manager of Manchester United. United had just played a game against York City and Tommy heard that they were looking for a manager. He immediately recommended me for the job. That's the kind of man he is. The fact that York City had the worst team in the league and I inherited a nightmare is beside the point. Mind you, he could have done me a bigger favour by NOT recommending me.

Something else he did was to make the ex-managers of United welcome at the ground. During his time there we always had an open invitation.

He's been through thick and thin, both inside football as well as outside. His well publicised affair with his present wife, who was then the wife of United's physio, culminated in his being sacked. When I took up the post of physio at Bury that caused me a few worries I can tell you!

He told Mary Brown he'd take her to places she'd never seen before. The first one was the Old Bailey! That was another time I bumped into him. I was in the lift and who should join me but the Doc. I said, 'Going down, Tom?' He replied, 'Aye, for three bloody years if I'm found guilty!'

Then there was the time he was dismissed by Altrincham. Believe me, no one gets dismissed by Altrincham! But Tommy did. He only got the job in the first place because the physio's wife was ugly!

He's now reached a stage where he's more successful as a speaker than he ever was in football. In fact, his speeches last longer than the time he spent at some clubs! But he'll always remain a character. Be it as a manager or an after dinner speaker.

THE DOC AND ME SHARING A JOKE. Or had he actually won a game

Derek Dougan

Wolves and Northern Ireland international, Derek also spent 13 years involved with the Professional Footballers Association.

I was responsible for employing the Doc for a lengthy time. About eight months to be precise. Well, it's lengthy when compared to most of the Doc's contracts.

Although we did have our ups and downs, he once accused me of being 'A legend in my own mind!' I could always enjoy the Doc's famous, if not caustic wit.

I'm sure that all his fans will be glad he's found a good substitute for football, and quite a few chairmen will be delighted by the fact.

And having read this latest book of his, I can see that he's enjoying life even more, although a night school course in English grammar might be advisable.

COULDN'T FIND A PHOTO OF JACK CHARLTON SO WE'VE USED BOBBY INSTEAD.

Jack Charlton

Jack Charlton has won 35 caps for England. A World Cup hero of 1966. Now the current manager of the Irish Republic.

One incident I'll never forget was a night before the Cup Final. We were staying at the same Hotel when I met Tommy and Paddy Crerand on their way out for a meal. They invited me along but I unfortunately had a prior engagement. So I wished them Bon Appetite. Neither had a clue what it meant.

The next morning I found them at breakfast and enquired how the night had gone. The Doc told me it was the most expensive meal he'd ever eaten. A hundred and fifty quids worth! I remarked it was going a bit even by his standards.

Then he explained they'd gone to a Greek restaurant and finished off the night in typical style by smashing plates. It seems that both he and Paddy had got a bit carried away and went through a whole stack of plates. What they didn't know at the time was that breakages were added to the bill. At fifty pence a plate!

I suppose that sums up Tommy Docherty. He never does anything by halves.

Peter Brackley

TV sports reporter and football commentator. Also one of the country's top after dinner speakers using a variety of impersonations.

I've never done an impression of Tommy Docherty. How can you exaggerate on a man who's larger than life already!

But what I have done is follow him at several dinners. It isn't the easiest thing in the world to do, but there are one or two advantages. First, you know that the atmosphere will be bubbling because of the Doc's reputation. Secondly, he is the perfect target for a spot of mickey taking.

When the person you are slagging off is actually present it's a bonus. It always makes the gag funnier. But the Doc's ability to laugh at himself makes it that bit easier.

We've appeared together at countless dinners. At a recent function I wasn't surprised to see Tommy there because he'd already told me he wasn't going.

Then there was the vacant job as England's cricket captain. One which Tommy rejected as it meant breaking his 5 hour contract with the Isle of Man Subbuteo team.

Then he went to Altrincham and was charged with bringing the game into disrepute! All because he went round telling people he was their football manager!

I look forward to appearing with the Doc many more times because one thing is certain. The punters know they're in for a good night.

Bob Russell
Daily Mirror Sports Correspondent

Tommy Docherty's rich, irrepressible if occasionally irreverent sense of humour knows few bounds.

It can be as cutting as a Claymore, as basic as his humble back-street Glasgow origins. It transcends at times to almost celestial heights!

The first time I realised that the Doc's rare, outrageous Scottish wit might be devinely inspired was on his maiden foreign trip as the new though hardly novice manager of Manchester United. We were in the Vatican.

The team and entourage — in Rome for an Anglo-Italian cup-tie — had been granted the honour of a private audience with the Pope.

As the party wended their way back to the hotel, quietly comparing their own particular experiences of a memorable afternoon the unmistakeable sound of Tommy Docherty in lighter mood cut through the lingering solemnity.

' Did ye see what happened when Mr McGoo (his name for a charming but short-sighted and rather senile United director) knelt to kiss the Papal ring? ', enquired T. D. half innocently, ' He missed! '

Then: 'And ye know what — the Pope was brilliant about it. All he said was he thought it was time we got ourselves a new goalkeeper.'

‘ Mind you it definitely was a bit darker than I expected in there! ’

The Doc wasn’t alone with the mirth and the mischief during those smiling seventies but he was always going to be a hard act to follow.

On another trip Lou Macari, United’s self-styled ‘prankster supreme’, decided that the best way of enjoying a Belgrade hotel that was more Alcatraz than your actual Hilton was by playing prison warder. And he did it well.

Nicking room keys, disconnecting telephones, making the chambermaid disappear had never been a problem with Lou. And in no time at all he had team-mates Gerry Daley and Paddy Roach all locked up with nowhere to go.

Tucked away in the sound-proof isolation of ‘Cell 607’ the two unsuspecting Irish lads finally settled down to a race-by-race re-run of their week old Sporting Life followed by a shared reading of the Yugoslav translation of the Eastern Episcopalian Book of Common Prayer.

Consequently they never made the social highspot of the tour, a magnificent dinner and evening out on the Yugoslav FA.

What made it the worse was their eventual discovery — about two hours too late — that crafty Macari, quiet as a mouse, had actually unlocked their ‘cell’ minutes before leaving with the rest of the team.

Worse still was the instant justice the Doc dished out at his late night ‘Star Chamber’ . . . seven days wages. Three days for AWOL, two for falsely accusing innocent team-mates and two for complaining to the press.

It was only when their wages went through ‘undocked’ that they realised that the prankster supreme had a rival.

Professional football can’t be all fun and games. As the late, great Anfield sage Bill Shankly once drolly declared: ‘ It’s not just life or death. It’s far more serious than that. ’

Yet even in the days when Liverpool had real live opposition, Tommy Docherty, with his refreshing, self-effacing attitude, always approached it on the bright side.

In his time at Old Trafford there was certainly never a dull moment . . . on or off the field.

SHALL WE DO THE SAME NEXT YEAR TOM?
DEPENDS IF I CAN MAKE ENOUGH MONEY TO PAY FOR YOUR LUNCHES!!!

THE END